THE CHURCH OUT ON A LIMERICK

ROB L. STAPLES

Illustrated by Rick Green

Beacon Hill Press of Kansas City
Kansas City, Missouri

Copyright 2000
by Beacon Hill Press of Kansas City

ISBN 083-411-8254

Printed in the
United States of America

Cover Design: Ted Ferguson and Rick Green

Library of Congress Cataloging-in-Publication Data

Staples, Rob L.
    The church out on a limerick / by Rob L. Staples ; illustrated by Rick Green.
      p. cm.
    ISBN 0-8341-1825-4
    1. Christian life—Humor. 2. Christianity—Humor. 3. Church—Humor. I. Title.

BV4517 .S75 2000
230'.002'07—dc21

                          00-059872

10   9   8   7   6   5   4   3   2   1

Dedication

To One who has not abdicated,
Who has always the sourpuss hated,
Whose great sense of humor
Is no idle rumor—
To God this dumb book's dedicated.

Contents

Preface

I spent 35 years teaching theology—13 years at the college level and 22 at a theological seminary. Along the way, I developed the hobby of composing limericks and would often throw one into my lectures, partly to illuminate the subject of the lecture, but mostly just to keep the students awake!

One year I noticed that a student in one of my courses always sat at the rear of the room and seemed to be diligently taking notes. Later I discovered that he was really drawing cartoons to depict what was being discussed. He was good. I made up my mind that if I ever put my limericks together into a book, I would ask this student to draw a cartoon to illustrate each one. His name was Rick Green. He is now a successful pastor known as Rev. Rick Green. Drawing these cartoons has provided him with some recreational escape from the demands of a busy parish life. My wife, Marcella, conceived the idea for the book's title and the kind of drawing Rick should create to adorn the cover.

When I was a full-time professor, I always felt a bit guilty spending time working on the limerick book when there were more academically acceptable things that needed to be done, such as lecture preparation, research, and serious writing. But happily I am now retired, and I have spent some of this retirement time putting this little book together, completely guilt-free.

A friend once wrote me: "Keep on laughing; it's better than bellyaching." He was doubtless giving a rough translation of Proverbs 17:22: "A cheerful heart is a good medicine, but a downcast spirit dries up the bones" (RSV).

Life would be miserable, and the world would be a sad place, if everyone, especially so-called religious folks, took themselves too seriously. A part of my calling is to stick pins into balloons of pomposity. A sizable amount of iconoclasm flows in my veins. You may find one of your idols smashed here. I trust the satirizing, spoofing, and lampooning carried on in these pages will be accepted for what they are meant to be—a prescription for the "good medicine" of laughter. If you cannot stomach that kind of medicine, or if you are a person who is easily offended when a little fun is poked at things you consider sacred, you should perhaps close the book and read no further. I would not wish to jeopardize your piety.

I have taught, and talked, about God during my entire career (that's what *theology* means, "God-talk"). But in our finite minds we cannot even begin to comprehend the infinite greatness of the Divine Being. Nevertheless, I am quite convinced of one thing: *God has a sense of humor.* With that conviction, this little book is presented. Have fun!

And now, dear reader, the sentence you are now reading is the last completely serious one in the book!

—Rob L. Staples

Introduction

I have always been fascinated by the names of churches. And I am often amused by the way preachers sometimes get themselves "out on a limb" in what they preach and promote.

One example of the latter that comes to mind was a religious paper that once got placed in my mailbox, along with some other junk mail such as an ad for carpet cleaning and a solicitation of my vote for the office of county tax assessor. It was one of those Bible prophecy productions on pulp paper, and it bore a July date. The lead article, by the paper's editor, predicted that the second coming of Christ would occur that September—just two months away. It was written so convincingly that for a few seconds I contemplated selling my possessions, dressing in a white robe, and looking for a mountaintop on which to await that blessed event.

Fortunately, before taking such rash action, I happened to glance at the back page of the publication before tossing it into the wastebasket. There the editor, the selfsame man who wrote that front-page article on the Second Coming, was advertising a trip to the Holy Land that he would lead in August, just one month away. The best part of the deal was the payment plan. Only a small deposit was required; the rest of the trip could be paid for in monthly installments over the next two years! Wow! One could not lose on a deal like that! Before having to pay up, we bargain-hunting pilgrims would be whisked away to that celestial abode where bill collectors (along with murderers, whoremongers, idolaters, and liars, according to Rev. 21:8) may not enter.

The juxtaposition of that editor's front-page piece on prophecy and his back-page ad for a Holy Land trip on the installment plan is what I call getting "out on a limb." Now this book contains none of that nonsense. Rather this book is designed to get you "out on a limerick." The messages printed on these pages are those that come straight from the church with the most interesting name I ever heard—*The Church Out on a Limerick.*

For those not familiar with the history, geography, and form of limericks, they originated once upon a time in the county of Limerick in Ireland. Obviously, that is why they are called limericks. They are humorous or nonsensical verses of five lines each. The rhyme scheme is *aabba.* (No, that is *not* a misspelling of the Aramaic word *abba,* which is found in the New Testament, loosely translated as "Father.") The rhyme scheme of *aabba* (you don't try to pronounce it, you just say the letters *a-a-b-b-a*) means this: The first, second, and fifth lines of the verse must rhyme with each other, and the third and fourth lines must rhyme with each other.

The whole verse is written in anapestic meter. Lines 1, 2, and 5 have three anapestic feet; and lines 3 and 4 have only two anapestic feet. The word *anapestic* comes from two Greek words and means "to strike back." This has nothing to do with the concept of retaliation (unless you want to get even with someone by reciting one of your limericks out loud!). An anapestic foot is made up of two short syllables followed by one long syllable. Thus, according to the dictionary, it is the opposite of a *dactyl.* I don't know what a dactyl is. But I once learned that a *pterodactyl* was a flying reptile that lived in the Jurassic period, the era of the dinosaurs. I suppose a dactyl could be either the ancestor or the offspring of a pterodactyl. As for a dactyl foot as used in poetry, the dictionary gives no clue, except to say it is a metrical foot, which is the opposite of an anapestic foot—which puts us right back where we started! This means that a dactyl foot is composed of one long syllable followed by two short ones. The dictionary does tell us that the word *dactyl* literally refers to a body part such as a finger or toe, that is, a digit. Maybe it refers to the foot of a flying reptile on which can be found three toes, one long one and two short ones. I am not sure.

But why bother with dactyl feet when we are really working here with anapestic ones? The dictionary defines an *anapest* as "a reversed dactyl." I assume that means an anapest is a flying reptile that walks, or flies, backward! It is a bit confusing.

As for limericks, which must have *anapestic* feet, I read somewhere (and I hope it is true) that in writing limericks, one is permitted to cheat a little. That is, you can drop or add a syllable as needed when you cannot make your syllables fit onto a perfect anapestic foot. At any rate, I have cheated some, I fear, in the following pages, by occasionally dropping or adding a syllable. And now and then, when I failed to be diligent, a *dactyl* toe seemed to grow on one of my *anapestic* feet! I hope I will be forgiven for such carelessness. At least I hope you will find the limericks entertaining enough not to be bothered by the cheating.

Although I confess to a little cheating regarding the use of anapestic feet, in the matter of plagiarism I plead 99 percent innocent. These limericks are my original compositions. That loophole of 1 percent is to give me cover in the unlikely event that somewhere in my past I heard a rhyme that got lodged in my subconscious and I forgot about hearing it, only to have it emerge years later, with perhaps some modification, as a verse of my own making. But I don't think I need the cover. I cannot remember ever being forgetful. If one of these limericks should sound like one you have heard before, perhaps you heard it from me. Or from someone who was quoting me.

The book is divided into six chapters. The lines of demarcation between the chapters are more like dotted lines than solid ones. There is some overlapping. For example, the "biblical" limericks in chapter 1 were the easiest. Consequently that is one of the longest chapters. Old Testament characters Noah and Jonah proved to be fruitful subjects. So fruitful, in fact, that I have placed in the last chapter a few of the rhymes inspired by those seagoing adventurers, just to keep the first chapter from getting too long. Heaven forbid that I should appear to be a radical biblicist!

Each chapter is introduced by an essay that reveals to the reader . . . uh . . . well . . . er . . . I am not sure what it reveals. Maybe just how utterly crazy I am.

Chapter 1

Biblical Hermetootics

As any divinity student knows, biblical hermeneutics, a subject taught in theological seminaries, is the science that deals with the interpretation of biblical texts. Biblical *hermetootics* is a similar science, but there are some significant differences. For one thing, it is *not* taught in theological seminaries, much to the shame of those institutions and the impoverishment of the church. Other differences can be seen by noting the derivation of the term.

The word *hermetootics* is formed by combining the word *hermetic* with the word *toot*. According to Webster (Noah, that is, not Daniel), *hermetic* refers to something "made perfectly airtight so that no gas or spirit can escape, as a hermetic seal."

The other part of the term *hermetootics* is the word *toot*, which is defined as "a short blast, as in tooting one's horn." According to Webster, it is probably a play on the slang expression "to wet one's whistle," which refers to a drinking spree or binge. According to the *Random House Dictionary*, *toot* in the German areas of Pennsylvania refers to "a paper bag." In Australia, the word means "toilet," a meaning strikingly appropriate, especially in that part of the continent known as the Outback.

Biblical hermetootics, then, is the science of opening up biblical stories, whose humor has hitherto been hermetically sealed, and allowing the "gas" or "spirit" of the story to escape, to the enjoyment of the readers of Holy Writ. Or, to put it another way, it is a methodology that allows these biblical stories to "toot" their horn in a way they have generally not been tooted by the more solemn pietistic readers of Scripture. Or, to put it still another way, the biblical "hermetoot" is the scholar who goes on an interpretative binge, locks himself in a toilet (as Descartes locked himself in a furnace room), meditates with his head in a paper bag, and finds things in Scripture that are not found by that lackluster sister science of mere "hermeneutics."

In the next pages are found some examples of the "assured results" of recent scholarship in biblical hermetootics, as the world's most famous "hermetoots" have interpreted the biblical accounts.

At the first we're told only that God
Created all things. It is odd
  That there isn't a clue
  (And I sure wish we knew)
What He stood on before He made sod!

Said a student who thought himself mod:
"I find it insulting that God,
    When He felt that He must
    Make a man, blew on dust,
Making me the offspring of a clod."

Baseball, to which sports fans are beckoned,
Is found in the Bible. 'Tis reckoned
   The root of our sinning,
   For in the Big Inning
Eve stole first, and Adam stole second.

When Adam had sinned and he knew it,
He claimed 'twas the woman who blew it.
    And Eve, out of luck,
    Likewise passed the buck
And said, "That old snake made me do it."

Gen. 6:6

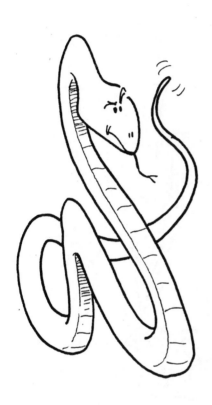

Surveying His work of creation,
God mused, "After much contemplation,
I do not repent
Five days that I spent,
But the sixth was a miscalculation."

Noah's ark had a problem for sure,
Which made voyaging hard to endure:
Just one vent in the top
And no good way to mop—
How on earth to dispose of manure?

Gen. 7
Noah probably wished he had
left some creatures behind.

Brother Noah was startled to hear
The sound that all ark captains fear.
So he gave the command,
"Hit the deck, every hand—
Bring those two blasted woodpeckers here!"

Gen. 19:26

The Lord clearly could not abide
The back glance of Lot's nosy bride.
Later, all that was found
Where she'd stood was a mound—
One part sodium and one part chloride.

Gen. 21:8–20
Did Hagar finally have the last laugh?

Which of Abraham's sons was the foil
For the other? The richest topsoil
　　Overlay Isaac's land.
　　Ishmael got desert sand
(Beneath which lay oceans of oil)!

Exod. 32:19

On Sinai, Moses heard (as God spoke 'em)
Ten Commandments in which was no hokum.
When he saw the gold calf,
What he did was no laugh.
He became the first one to have broke 'em.

Miss Rahab, who ran a bordello,
Had entertained many a fellow.
    On two spies she took pity
    Who told her, "This city
Soon will look like a stepped-on marshmallow!"

Judg. 16
Long hair was never meant just for hippies!

Samson's strength and great body condition
Would be lauded by any physician.
    But the man was a nut
    When he got his hair cut
By Delilah, that ancient beautician.

Goliath was full of palaver,
Bloodthirsty, his mouth drooling slaver.
At the peak of his wrath,
This giant from Gath
Became a beheaded cadaver.

2 Sam. 11:1–5
(And he didn't even have binoculars!)

When King David peeked over the wall,
The view fairly made his chin fall!
*   (Bathsheba in bubbles!)*
*   He did not shun troubles.*
His libido became his downfall.

The den was the strongest of bastions,
And the lions weren't Simbas or Aslans.
But the ones in that lair
Ne'er laid paw on Dan's hair,
Nor became the predicted assassins.

When Jonah refused God's suggestion,
A whale had a unique ingestion.
Saying, "Jonah, come off it,"
It swallowed the prophet,
Then suffered acute indigestion.

Chapter 2

Hecklesiastical Hackademia

As everyone knows, the word *academia* refers to the academic world of scholarship, research, and learning. The word *hackademia* has a similar meaning, but there are some significant differences that can be seen by noting the derivation of the term.

The word *hackademia* is formed by combining the word *academia* with the word *hack*. Hack is both a verb and a noun. As a verb, hack means "to chop or cut roughly as with a hatchet." It may also refer to the physical reflex of coughing, especially when the cough is a harsh and dry one.

As a noun, hack can mean either "an old, worn-out horse" or "a person hired to do dull, routine work." All these meanings seem to be incorporated into the word *hackademia.* It is that realm of scholarly activity where the dull, routine work of chopping and cutting up students is done by worn-out old horses with dry, harsh coughs.

The modifier, *hecklesiastical,* is distantly related to the word *ecclesiastical,* which denotes that which is connected to the church, hence "churchly." *Hecklesiastical* has a similar meaning, but there are some significant differences. The word is formed by combining the word *heckle* with the word *ecclesiastical.* The word *heckle* means "to annoy or harass a speaker by interrupting with questions or taunts." In turn, heckle is based on the root word *heck,* which is often uttered by people who are overly pious and feel a little squeamish about using four-letter words that are biblical, preferring to get their four-letter words from nonbiblical sources, as when a preacher exhorts, "If you don't repent, you'll go to heck."

Hecklesiastical hackademia, therefore, denotes that world

of church-sponsored educational institutions (such as colleges, universities, and seminaries) where students heckle their teachers (those coughing and worn-out old horses) by taunts and interruptions, while those worn-out old horses perform the dull routine work of chopping up the students at grade time.

**Some skills aren't taught in seminary
but have to be learned on the job!**

*Just before service time, Reverend Bell
(Forbidding the janitor to tell)
        Turned the heat up (how dirty!)
        To a hundred and thirty,
Before preaching his sermon on hell.*

The progress of learning!

There once was a student named Guesser
Whose knowledge grew lesser and lesser.
It soon grew so small
He knew nothing at all,
And now he's a college professor.

**Some professorships should be avoided
by everyone but healthy persons.**

*His fever was a hundred and two.
The poor chap had a bad case of flu.
He's a fine Ph.D.
But embarrassed, for he
Teaches faith healing at O.R.U.*

Students really ought to do their assignments.

A student with brain somewhat rattlely
Did not do the reading collaterally
        That the prof had assigned.
        Though he griped and he whined,
He was flunked by the prof unilaterally.

**Some preachers seek hungrily
for those honorary degrees.**

*Honorary degrees, for fame cravers,
Come in all sorts of colors and flavors.
They're all over the place.
They are gifts of God's grace,
Which means they're unmerited favors.*

Divinity students who study hard to earn degrees often joke about preachers who sport those honorary doctor of divinity (D.D.) designations that require little or no work.

DR. RICH E. OUS, D.D.

Said a student one day in the quad:
"I find it exceedingly odd
    That some preachers, with ease,
    End their name with two Ds,
While one is sufficient for GOD."

Honorary degrees have puffed up many a preacher.

Pastor Fiddle received a degree.
He was thrilled and his heart sang with glee.
    He's so proud of his fame
    That he now signs his name
"The Reverend Fiddle, D.D."

The doctor of ministry degree was not meant to prepare one to leave the pastoral ministry.

One pastor (and he has much kin)
Decided to get a D.Min.,
*   Then gave up his preaching*
*   And got a job teaching,*
Much to his committee's chagrin.

Romance sometimes diminishes a student's G.P.A.

His exam grade could not have been worse,
And for this he showed little remorse.
    He, in love, was elated.
    Each night he had dated,
With the heart put ahead of the course.

The results of goofing off at examination time

A great many college professors
Have students who often are guessers,
Who won't do their best
To prepare for a test.
Later, profs become father confessors.

Chapter 3

Church Histrionics

Church history is a discipline taught in most theological seminaries. It deals with the development of the institution and the teachings of the Christian church. *Church histrionics* is a similar discipline, but there are significant differences.

According to the dictionary, the term *histrionics* (noun, singular or plural) refers to the theatrical arts. A second meaning is "exaggerated emotional behavior calculated for effect." The adjective *histrionic* relates to actors and acting. A second meaning is "excessively dramatic or emotional."

So there you have it. *Church histrionics* refers to those actors in the church who have displayed certain talents for the dramatic and emotional on the stage of history. The following pages will display some of the dramatic and emotional outbursts, and a little of the thinking of these actors.

Welcome, then, to *Church Histrionics 101.*

It has been said that the blood of the martyrs is the seed of the Church. Of course Socrates lived (and died) before there was a Church.

They killed the great Savonarola,
Burned Hus (some distrusted Loyola),
Put John on Patmos rock,
Gave Socrates hemlock,
Which did not affect him like a Cola.

One of the great church fathers could never quite rid his mind of the idea that Adam's fall, and thus humanity's predicament, was rooted in sexual desire.

St. Augustine thought he had found
The sin by which mankind is bound:
*   "It was not," so said he,*
*   "The apple in the tree,*
But the lust of the 'pair' on the ground."

The patriarch of Constantinople so separated the divine and human natures of Christ as to virtually make them separate persons.

His name once became quite notorious
For views of Christ thought quite inglorious.
"Christ was a duality—
A split personality,"
Said Constantinople's Nestorius.

**There were some great theologians
in the late Middle Ages.**

*Anselm, Abelard, and Aquinas—
Great medieval men who incline us
   Of their deep thoughts to drink.
   Were they here, I would think
We'd love to have them wine and dine us.*

"It's the economy, stupid. Money is needed to finish St. Peter's Basilica in Rome," said one John Tetzel.

The church Martin Luther did scold,
For the many indulgences sold.
That huckster, old Tetzel,
Twisted faith like a pretzel,
To rake in some building fund gold.

Martin Luther's Ninety-five Theses ignited a Reformation.

The indulgence sale vexed Luther sore,
And he angrily screamed and he swore:
"I'll tear Rome to pieces!
I'll write up some theses
And post them to The Wittenberg Door."

"Simul justus et peccator"—Latin for "At once both righteous and sinner," Martin Luther's description of the Christian.

"Martin Luther," said Rome's Holy Father,
"To the church you're a terrible bother.
You're no saint, that's for sure,
And I say that you're
Much less simul justus than peccator."

Chapter 4

Fun-de-mentalism and Libel-ism

One of the most interesting chapters in the history of American Christianity is the controversy in the early part of the 20th century between the Fundamentalists and the liberals. Within the pages of the present work, I refuse to take sides in that debate.

In fact, there is hardly any resemblance between that church-splitting debate and this chapter. Fundamentalism and Fun-de-mentalism are two different things, in spite of the fact that some have thought they were both nonintellectual, that is, "de-mental."

And there is no basic difference between Liberalism and Libel-ism, although some people in the religious right have felt they were being libeled in liberal schools, churches, and the press, as the debates among Southern Baptists bear witness. Those people see themselves as the "religious wronged."

No, here we do not distinguish between Fun-de-mentalism and Libel-ism. Depending upon one's viewpoint, Fun-de-mentalism and Libel-ism may be seen as synonymous, the former being libelous and the latter being de-mental.

The only purpose here is to have some "fun" with certain aspects of the religious scene that may be described as "de-mental," even though some readers may think such fun is libel. Any who think that way are asked to go back and read the dedication page in this book.

Well, <u>some</u> books on the Rapture sell quite well!

Somewhere in his third or fourth chapter,
The author predicted the Rapture.
But the date came and went.
Now he can't pay the rent,
With his landlord demanding his ouster.

The Book of Jonah (a tale of a whale and a whale of a tale)

"I believe it, though it's quite a tale,"
Said the pious but wise Brother Dale,
"But my faith would be dead
If the Bible had said
That Jonah had swallowed a whale!"

Gen. 4:9 in reverse

One monkey opined to another:
"Humans say we are kin to each other;
*   If true, evolution*
*   Engenders pollution.*
I'm ashamed to be my keeper's brother."

Taking the Bible too literally might produce a strange piety.

R. GREEN

A literalist in black judgment frock
Said, "The liberals our faith do much mock."
　　Then he went out alone
　　And prayed to a stone,
For he'd read in the Psalms, "God's a Rock."

The subject of Bible prophecy worries some folks.

Poor old Sister Hortense McKenzie!
She worked herself into a frenzy
About Satan's live birth
On the great planet Earth.
She'd better stop reading Hal Lindsey.

Dry spells can affect baptismal practices— or can they?

The west Texas drought made things dry.
Streams dried up, cattle started to die.
Baptists tried a new wrinkle
And started to sprinkle!
(Now you know that this verse is a lie.)

Pastors should make sure some announcements are inerrant.

He announced on the church's marquee
He'd be preaching on "Inerancy."
But it looked quite absurd,
For he misspelled the word.
He now runs a State Farm agency.

"Give me liberty or give me death," said Patrick Henry, another famous spellbinder from Virginia.

Down in Lynchburg on each Sunday morn
J. Falwell takes the bull by the horn,
Rings his Liberty bell,
Warning folks about hell,
Liberals, Democrats, smut, and porn.

Chapter 5

Contemptowary Theology

Contemptowary theology is a little like "contemporary theology," but there are some significant differences. The origin of the term *contemptowary* is somewhat obscure, and there are differing theories regarding its derivation. It is generally agreed, however, that words ending in "wary" usually connote something of which one needs to "beware" (i.e., "be wary"). Thus contemptowary in this context would designate a theological viewpoint of which one should be wary.

It is not at all certain whether the first part of the word (the Latin *contempto*) derives from *contemporary, contemplation,* or *contemptible.* But many reputable scholars believe it partakes of elements from all three. Thus the term *contemptowary theology* suggests that the theology bearing this designation is up-to-date ("contemporary"), but when we "contemplate" it, we should be wary, for it is "contemptible." However, it is possible that the word was originally formed simply by joining the words *contempt* and *wary,* with the connecting letter *o* inserted for euphonic purposes.

Although the above opinions have been widespread and enduring, in recent times a new hypothesis has been put forth. According to this theory, *contemptowary* is formed by joining *contempt* to the last half of *cassowary.* The latter is the name of a large bird that looks something like an ostrich (the bird that buries its head in the sand) and is related to the emu. The natural habitat of these birds is Australia, New Guinea, and other "down under" islands of the South Pacific. Contemptowary theology, therefore, represents a theological perspective considered by Fundamentalists to be upside down. Another point made by some theologians is that this bird does not like the sunshine, preferring to build its nest in dark places. "Aha," cries the Fundamentalist, "such theology cannot stand the light of day!" This fact is counterbalanced, however, by another: This bird has three toes on each foot, apparently signifying a *Trinitarian* theology. This, it would seem, ought to satisfy the demands of even the most demanding conservatives. Some have gone so far as to suggest that Trinitarianism is also symbolized by the fact that there are three letters in the word *emu,* the bird family to which the cassowary is related.

Probably the most theologically significant characteristic of the cassowary bird is its inability to fly. It can only walk (and, if scared, run). "Aha," says the Fundamentalist, "contemptowary theology doesn't have a leg to stand on . . . er . . . ah . . . I mean, a wing to fly with."

Old Testament scholars are familiar with the documentary hypothesis, which posits four different sources of the Pentateuch (the first five books of the Bible), designated as J, E, D, and P. In similar vein, this hypothesis (that *contemptowary* comes from the words *contempt* and *cassowary*) is sometimes called the "cockumentary hypothesis," coming as it does from the name of a large bird. There is no evidence, however, that it is a *male* bird. It could have been female, but still, we know of no attempt to name this theory the *"hen*umentary hypothesis."

Furthermore, just as the documentary hypothesis is sometimes called the JEDP theory, the cockumentary hypothesis is often referred to as the CADD theory, which is an acronym for "Cock-A-Doodle-Do."

At any rate, this theory deserves to be examined carefully. Although we prefer the more conservative view that the term *contemptowary* is simply the joining of the words *contempt* and *wary,* with the letter *o* inserted for euphonic purposes, we have to admit that the cockumentary hypothesis seems to be attested by an obscure piece of ancient poetry that has been unearthed by archaeologists in the caves of Cumcrawld, located near the Live Ocean. This piece of poetry is one of the famous "Live Ocean Scrolls," which have revolutionized theological research in recent decades. It seems to have been written by some extremely conservative sect and reads as follows:

> *The bird with the name cassowary*
> *Has handicaps that are quite scary.*
> *Till the day it must die*
> *It cannot ever fly—*
> *Like viewpoints called contemporary.*

You will have noticed, dear reader, that this introductory essay on contemptowary theology is longer than the introductions to the other chapters. To compensate for the time you have spent reading it, I have placed fewer limericks in this section than in any of the others, for which I am sure you will be grateful.

Actually the motive was not all that altruistic. With the subject matter of this chapter being a bit more abstract, it was more difficult to compose limericks that could be illustrated with a cartoon. And for that, Rick is grateful!

One ancient philosopher believed the only unchanging reality was change itself.

Heraclitus gave expert advice,
And in spurning it one pays a price,
For it's still a safe bet
He would think you all wet
If you stepped in the same river twice!

Philosopher A. N. Whitehead is the patron saint of the process theologians.

Whitehead says God turns over a page
And each moment begins a new stage,
Grows wiser and older!
But we need His shoulder,
And we hope He won't die of old age!

Two giant early 20th-century theologians were Karl Barth of Basel and Emil Brunner of Zurich. They disagreed some and seldom met.

From Basel to Zurich it's clear
That as distances go, they're quite near.
But to E. Brunner's line
Karl Barth replied, "Nein!"
And they ne'er got together for beer.

Two same-name designers—Calvin Klein of fashion and John Calvin of theology.

Calvin Klein raised his assets and means,
Sewed his name on the back of some jeans
Sold to guy and to gal.
But Switzerland's Cal
Sewed "original sin" in the genes.

German theologian Jürgen Moltmann was one of the chief architects of the theology of hope.

A student of Moltmann was moping,
And hope against hope he was hoping
He could master the scope
Of those teachings on hope,
And wasn't quite sure he was coping.

On Dietrich Bonhoeffer

Bonhoeffer wrote page after page
About man who is now come of age.
    We have grown up quite well,
    Yet one never can tell
When we may just go through one more stage.

For a person who was not a theologian,
Clive Staples Lewis was a good theologian!
The most important influence in his life
was the preacher George MacDonald.

C. S. Lewis sure did have a knack
For going to heaven and back
  By means of his fiction
  In which his depiction
Of sin he had learned from "Big Mac."

Nothing can defeat the power of positive thinking.

It gives us some positive feelings
To know we can make some good dealings,
That the key to success
Lies within one's own breast.
Give us more of dear Norm Vincent's pealings!

Roman Catholic theologians do not always get the pope's blessing.

Hans Kung, the famed Catholic scholar,
Caused Rome to cry "foul" and to holler
When he just could not see
Infallibility
But saw specks on the papal white collar.

Chapter 6

Concluding Unpietistic Postscript
(With apologies to Kierkegaard)

The famous 19th-century Danish philosopher Søren Kierkegaard, known in the history of philosophy as "the melancholy Dane," was perhaps the first outstanding exponent of existentialism. He once wrote a treatise with the interesting title *Concluding Unscientific Postscript*. Actually, its full title was *Concluding Unscientific Postscript to the "Philosophical Fragments."* The *Philosophical Fragments* was an earlier work of his, to which the *Postscript* was tacked on as something of an explanation. That explains why he called it a *Concluding* postscript, even though the term *Concluding... Postscript* is something of a tautology. I am not sure why he even bothered to call it *Unscientific*. It seems obvious enough that he was writing philosophy rather than science. But if you want to know his real reason for calling it *Unscientific*, you will have to go read the Dane himself; I don't have the time or the space here (and possibly not the intelligence either) to try to explain it.

Now, dear reader, if you think all this has anything to do with this book of limericks, you are woefully mistaken. It merely led me to play on Mr. K's title and call this part of the book *Concluding Unpietistic* (rather than unscientific) *Postscript*. I have called it a *Postscript* because it was conceived after the other chapters were already designated. I have called it *Concluding* because it is the last chapter in the book. Wasn't that brilliant of me? And it is *Unpietistic* because ... well ... er ...

because it just is. But that should be no surprise. Everything in this book is unpietistic.

In this chapter I have poked a little fun at anything that came to mind where it seemed that a little iconoclasm would be good for the individual's (and the church's) soul.

Actually, to be perfectly honest, my purpose was not that noble. This chapter was devised as a good place to dump all those limericks that I had fun writing but that did not seem to fit into any of the other five chapters. Even a few "biblical" ones were placed here because, unlike those in chapter 1, they were not based on a specific chapter or verse. Now you know.

God works in mysterious ways.

Said a monk: "What a craftsman was God!
Took male rib, made a whole female bod,
And then fashioned her fate,
Making her a blind date
With a dude He had made from some sod."

Being pastor of a "crystal cathedral" like the one in southern California definitely has its hazards.

Preachers in a glass church have an inkling
They mustn't throw stones, start glass tinkling.
(Just ask Doctor Schuler;
There's nobody cooler.)
It's called "possibility thinkling."

Hedonism, from the Greek <u>hedone</u> (pleasure),
is the pursuit of or devotion to pleasure
(one view of the fall).

Eve and Adam, whose world was primeval,
Ruined the world (ancient, mod, and medieval),
　　Setting up, east of Eden,
　　A Garden of Hedon.
Now our world's one of "Atom" and "Evil."

Being a passenger on the ark was no Caribbean pleasure cruise! But the vessel could have been worse!

Noah's sons thought the old man was manic.
'Twas enough to cause strong men to panic.
Sleep on hay? Feed on oats?
Like the donkeys and goats?
But at least they weren't on the Titanic!

Bad things can happen when one becomes stir-crazy.

Feeling tired, exhausted, and weak,
As the trip became boring and bleak,
    Noah got a great scare
    When he had a nightmare
And dreamed that the ark sprang a leak!

Environmental pollution on Noah's ark

Safe on board, Captain Noah said, "Well,
The seas are beginning to swell,
    But the worst of my woes,
    (An offense to my nose),
Is this terrible animal smell!"

Could so many come from just two?

One housewife, I hear, oft reproaches
A pest that so slyly encroaches
    In her kitchen not purely
    Kept clean: "Noah surely
Took on the ark more than two roaches!"

One more about Noah's ark

Noah's sons were not easy to please
As they scratched and could not sleep with ease,
And they asked of their dad
Why he'd done what he had
And allowed on the ark those two fleas.

A time warp: the movie
<u>The Ten Commandments</u> in reverse

Moses prayed, when he saw the Red Sea,
"Lord, have You some guidance for me?"
God said, "Read Instructions
For Meeting Obstructions.
Look under 'DeMille, Cecil B.'"

Being a missionary can sometimes have its downside.

The cannibal tribe showed its ire,
Tasting priest from the pot on the fire.
He made terrible steak!
They had made a mistake
And had boiled him. But he was a friar!

Call them the "Champaign Gospel Music Makers."
A one, and a two, and a . . .

Nashville's gospel music big business
Makes one reel with big money dizziness.
There is dough to be had.
Now the songs aren't all bad
If one has the taste for such fizziness.

Don't pray too loudly when wearing false teeth.

The pastor, while praying the prayer,
Sneezed his dentures out into the air,
And down in the front pew,
Waving hand, sat Jane Drew.
She's recovered them out of her hair!

"Out of the mouth of babes and sucklings" (Ps. 8:2; Matt. 21:16).

My daughter at our dinner table
Asked a question I still am unable
To answer: "At the start,
Did God, who was smart,
Give Adam, the first man, a navel?"

Oh, the things that can go wrong at weddings!

At a wedding once held in Toledo
The dad wore a rented tuxedo.
　　But too tight on the hip
　　The pants gave a loud rip,
And the ring boy thought that was real neato.

Some pastoral counseling situations could present a problem with the tenth commandment.

Though skillful and having ability,
Some things were beyond his facility,
Like the man who confessed,
(Getting guilt off his chest),
That he coveted his neighbor's humility.

Telling it like it is.

Railed a preacher to his congregation:
"It's my candid and clear observation,
That for all you've professed,
When you're put to the test,
You resist anything but temptation!"

Don't bury a man until you are sure he is dead!

Just before they closed Gramp's casket lid,
His feet were touched by Grandson Sid:
    "He still has body heat;
    No one dies with warm feet!"
Just then Grandpa moaned: "Joan of Arc did."

The church secretary's nightmare

The computer she would not espouse
When installed in the new parish house,
*   And she screamed and complained*
*   When the salesman explained*
*That attached to the thing was a **mouse**!*

Fallen angels in the children's Christmas pageant?

The play dramatizing Christ's birth
Lost all semblance of order and mirth
*   When the angels that night*
*   Got embroiled in a fight*
Over which one would sing "Peace on Earth."

How do you spell <u>relief?</u> (Those written announcements should be spell-checked.)

The church supper was really a dilly,
But the poster put up by Aunt Millie
On the bulletin board
Had one misspelled word:
"We'll have tacos and bow<u>e</u>ls of chili."

The Lord's Prayer in a technological age

That cute little girl, Abigail,
Said her prayer every night without fail
(Such sweet contemplation!):
"Lead us not to temptation,
But deliver us from the E-mail."

Don't let this be the end!

Of these pages you've come to the last,
But we hope your fun isn't all past.
 We must now say "good-bye,"
 But please don't let time fly
Without laughing and having a blast.